S T U



# Come Out de Wilderness

## A BIBLE STUDY BASED ON AFRICAN AMERICAN SPIRITUALS

DARCEL HOLLOWAY

*Abingdon Press/Nashville*

COME OUT DE WILDERNESS: A BIBLE STUDY BASED ON AFRICAN AMERICAN SPIRITUALS, STUDENT BOOK

Marilyn Thornton, Development Editor



This book is printed on acid-free, elemental-chlorine-free paper.

Library of Congress Cataloging-in-Publication Data
ISBN 0-687-32553-3



The art on the cover is Coming to Jones Road #7: We Jus' Keep A Comin' (2000) by Faith Ringgold. She is a highly decorated artist, known for her painted story quilts. Her awards include the Guggenheim Fellowship for painting, two from the National Endowment, and the Coretta Scott King Award. Her works can be seen at the New York Museum of Modern Art, Studio Museum in Harlem, the Guggenheim Museum, and The Metropolitan Museum of Art.

05 06 07 08 09 10 11 12 13 14 — 10 9 8 7 6 5 4 3 2
MANUFACTURED IN THE UNITED STATES OF AMERICA

# Contents

"Can' tell you how many times I done heard that text preached on. They always tell the slaves dat ef he be good an' worked hard fo' his master, dat he would go to heaven, an' dere he gonna live a life of ease. They ain' never tell him he gonna be free in Heaven. You see, they didn't want slaves to start thinkin' bout freedom, even in Heaven."

(Beverly Jones, ex-slave)

"De songs wuz old Negro spirituals sung in de deep rich voice of our race. We didn't hab no songbooks, nor couldn't read if we had 'em. We sorter made 'em up, as us went 'long."

(Steve Weathersby, ex-slave)

# Introduction

We is gathered hyeah, my brothers, in dis howlin' wilderness
Fu' to speak some words of comfo't to each othah in distress.

From An Antebellum Sermon by Paul Laurence Dunbar

*Come Out de Wilderness: A Bible Study Based on African American Spirituals* is the fourth in an adult resource series that examines the connection between the experience of African American slaves and biblical literature as found in African American spirituals. (*Plenty Good Room* Fall 2002, *Mary Had a Baby* Fall 2003, and *Ride On, Jesus* Spring 2004) Additionally, it is the adult component to *Shouting in the Hush Arbor: Celebrate God in Community!*

The record is plain. Despite the efforts of many white Christians to either completely exclude them by withholding the gospel, or to enslave spirit and mind as well as body by preaching a tainted, racist gospel in segregated worship settings, pre-Civil War African Americans sought God in the wilderness, creating the "invisible institution" whereby they could worship the Lord "in Spirit and in truth." The introductory excerpt is from a poem by Paul Laurence Dunbar (1872–1906), an American writer whose parents had been enslaved. It is a rhymed tribute to the determination of a people who knew a God of freedom despite the constant preaching to "obey masters" heard in the church houses and services of mainstream Christianity. They called these wilderness places brush arbors, hush harbors, or hush arbors.

The hush arbor is a real event in American history. The Christian community, black and white, often met in brush arbors—woodsy places—to hold revivals and camp meetings. The Second Great Awakening Revival Movement of the early nineteenth century witnessed many such events. The hush arbor or hush harbor, however, was particular to the slave community.

There are many accounts of slaves, adults with their children, slipping into the woods, into swamps or gullies at night, to have worship services where they could pray for freedom and salvation. The slaves would break tree branches to signify meeting places. Huddling together, they conducted meetings where they could feel the presence of God away from the eyes and ears of the slave owner.

Consider the story of Henry Evans, who left southeastern Virginia in 1775. Evans was a cobbler by trade, African American by birth, and Methodist by denomination. On his way to Charleston, South Carolina, he got to Fayetteville, North Carolina, where he was astounded by the lack of spiritual nurture of the slaves and free Blacks like himself. He could not go on to Charleston until he preached the Gospel of Jesus Christ. His compelling preaching soon attracted crowds, and to stop him the local city officials banned him from preaching there.

Under the conviction that he must preach, he moved the meetings to the wooded sand hills. Flameless beds of coals were spread in pits and whole hogs were cooked for those who could slip away at night for preaching meeting. Word got out, and the white folks began to search for their location to break up the meetings. On one of those searches they came upon a clearing, freshly "tromped down." What they discovered was a hastily abandoned pit with a whole hog, fully cooked, that was hardly touched. The vigilante searchers tried the meat because it smelled so good. It was wonderfully delicious. Not long after this, the white citizens of Fayetteville had a change of heart. A church was built for Mr. Evans in Fayetteville, and years later a retirement home was established for this cobbler and lay preacher.*

For most black Christians enduring slavery, however, worship continued to be a secret and dangerous affair. Being "hushed" was imperative. If someone was overcome by sorrow or joy at one of these secret meetings, an iron pot turned upside down was used to "catch" the sound. They called this "shoutin' in the pot." New converts were covered with quilts as the community sang. The hush arbor is where the preacher and people could call and respond in ways that originated in Africa and where the Negro Spiritual came to life.

*Come Out de Wilderness* is the title of one of the spirituals included in this Bible study. The origins of the text revolve around the historical figure, Denmark Vesey (c.1767–1822), leader of a slave insurrection in South Carolina. Vesey was a carpenter. He purchased his freedom in 1800. He was first a Presbyterian and then became a member of the AME church. He preached rebellion against slavery on plantations within 100 miles of Charleston. At his house people gathered and gave money for the purchase of arms. The uprising was planned for June of 1822 but the conspiracy was betrayed. Denmark Vesey fled into the woods. Upon his capture, he was asked, "How did you feel when you come out de wilderness?" Vesey answered, "I'm just leaning on de Lord." Vesey was hanged on July 3, 1822, along with 35 conspirators.

The wilderness worship experience of the African American slave represented a resistance to chattel slavery. The creation of spirituals like those included in this study shows the resilience of the human spirit as it reaches out to the God of Creation, Deliverance, and Love. In the wilderness—the hush arbor—despite their precarious situation, the people could feel the safety of God's love in a community of faith.

As you study the lessons in *Come Out de Wilderness: A Bible Study Based on African American Spirituals* remember that God is with you no matter your situation or circumstance. Our slave ancestors witnessed to this understanding through song and by their actions. From "Joshua Fit de Battle of Jericho" to "Little David Play on Your Harp" to "De Blind Man," they show us how they learned and taught the Bible. From the singing of "My God Is So High" to "Come Out de Wilderness" they reveal to us a faith in a God that had never left them yet! So even in the midst of an enslaved existence they could ask, "Did you love ev'rybody when you come out de wilderness?" Like Vesey, let us continue to lean on the Lord.

— *Marilyn E. Thornton*
*The editor*

* April 30 Sermon: "A Proud Remnant—A Legacy of Faith" by Bishop Charlene P. Krammer, North Carolina area. (at www.UMC.org 2004)

## Lesson 1

# My God Is So High

Psalm 139:1-12, 17-18

**Key Verse**
"Where can I go from your spirit?
Or where can I flee from your presence"? (Psalm 139:7)

**Theme**
Celebrate faith in a God that is always present.

**African Proverb**
One may go around a river or around a hill
but one cannot go around God.

**Word**
Present

***"My God Is So High"***
**Chorus**

My God is so high, you can't get over him
He's so low, you can't get under him
He's so wide, you can't get around him
You must come in by and through the Lamb

**Verse**

One day as I was walking, along the heavenly road
My Savior spoke unto me and filled my heart with his love

**Verse**

I'll take my gospel trumpet and I'll begin to blow
And if my Savior helps me, I'll blow wherever I go

## *Let's Listen: A Song of Sustaining Faith*

Celebrating the depth and breath of a God so enormous and all encompassing, "My God Is So High" explains that one cannot measure how high, how deep or how wide God's being stretches. If we travel the entire circumference of the earth or even the total expanse of the universe, still God's being would be immeasurable. With this welcomed dilemma comes the wonderful assurance that whatever the size of the problem or whatever the difficulty of the circumstance, as the old cliché says, "There's nothing too hard for God." Why is this so? According to this spiritual, it's because, "God is so high, you can get over him; so low, you can't get under him; (and) so wide, you can't get around him."

The theology of this old African American spiritual says that this is why we needed a Savior. The lyrics proclaim, "You must come in by and through the Lamb." The lamb spoken of in the song is Jesus the Christ and the literal meaning of his name is the Anointed One Who Saves. Christ was God incarnate, taking on human form to become "Emmanuel," meaning "God with us." God sent Jesus the Son into the world to be a vehicle of reconciliation between God and God's people. This great Creator of the Universe allowed the people intimate contact with their God through Jesus Christ. This was cause for celebration as enslaved Africans sang of their wonderful and all powerful God who brought liberation in the midst of their predicament as victims of chattel slavery in a new world.

Today this spiritual is sung in churches everywhere in celebration of a God whose goodness, mercy, and power has no equal. The rhythmic and melodic emphasis of the chorus is on the word "so," illustrating the indescribable quality of infinite God's presence. The lyrics of the first verse show the necessity of the believer having an experience with God. God is so high, so low, and so wide but not too big to touch the individual. God's love fills the individual in such a way that the news of such love must be shared. The second verse declares the goal of sharing the gospel message loud and clear, blowing it on a trumpet in every time and situation. God is experienced intra-personally and interpersonally, within the self and in community. There is also the assurance that God will help believers as they go. What a joyful expression of God's love and grace!

Many critics have said that Christianity was given to enslaved Africans to tame them; yet, when one examines their music it is evident that instead it served to sustain them. Their own understanding of God can be seen in this African proverb: "One may go around a river or around a hill but one cannot go around God." As a result, many Africans made the choice to take on Christianity and make it their own. They consequently developed a spiritual genius that caused them to survive the evils of slavery and at the same time give birth to the black religious experience in America.

**"We had dem spirit-filled meetings at night on de bank of de river, and God met us dere. We was quiet 'nuf' so de white folks didn't know we was dere, and what a glorious time we did have in de Lord."**
**(Susan Rhodes, ex-slave)**

The African American spiritual became an important source of inspiration and support, which resulted in a clever tool of communication. In quiet but spirited worship deep in the woods of the hush arbor, these transplanted Africans celebrated their faith and belief in God as their hope and peace. Though their mouths spoke in a "hush," their spirits rejoiced in exuberant worship. Sometimes they had to speak in silence, like a quiet storm. Although their voices were quieted, their hearts were filled with Holy Ghost shouts. Though their bodies were enslaved, their minds were free. They were free to celebrate their wholeness, free to hope for their future and free to believe in a God great enough to allow them to someday overcome their circumstances. Their God was at once, high and deep and wide enough to will it so.

In a sermon, the Rev. David Forbes, senior minister of Martin Street Baptist Church in Raleigh, North Carolina, said that the brilliance of that worship came from the uniting of hope, pain, oppression and suffering. "In order to appreciate the soul that ushers forth in our worship, its rhythms, sounds and the release, one must be in touch with the fact our faith reflects our experience. When you blend suffering, with faith, hope and the expectation of victory, then you have a context for African American worship." These elements characterize the familiar "shout" that can be found in some African American churches. Shouting in the hush arbor became the vehicle that not only worked out their salvation but also caused them to practice their faith in a meaningful and life sustaining way.

## *An Inescapable Spirit: Psalm 139:1-6; 17-18*

Psalm 139 is a psalm of lament by David. The lament functions to move the congregation or individual from crisis to triumph. The psalmist expects deliverance, comfort, and assurance that God is always present and knows everything! The psalmist makes a confession or complaint to God, affirms his trust in God, makes a request for intervention, and concludes with a blessing. David begins with a revelatory confession. "O LORD, you have searched me and known me." The word search means to pierce or bore—as one would bore a hole into the ground. David writes as if God had performed a thorough examination on him. God's thorough knowledge is directly linked to God's creation of him. To illustrate the totality of God's knowledge, the psalmist expresses the fact that God knows his every movement, motive, and moment (verses 2-3). God's knowledge is infinite and has no boundaries. There is a limit, however, to humanity (You hem me in). Nevertheless, God understands and knows all about humans, their strengths and weaknesses. God is omniscient, all-knowing.

In other words, "God is so high, you can't get over him, so low, you can't get under him and so wide, you can't get around him." In knowing that God is constantly searching him out, David expresses a lament because he was aware of his sinful nature. Nevertheless, he knew that even as God would hold him accountable for his sins, God still loved him. God was with David through the good, the bad, and the ugly, and God is with us in every circumstance. Even in places that seem absent of the knowledge and presence of God, whether the holding pen of a slave fort or ship, in the wilderness places of a new land; whether in rough inner-city streets, parentless homes, or inadequate schools, God's love and power are always available. God knows and God cares.

**When we think with the mind of God, we can begin to think outside the box and focus on the awesomeness of God within us.**

In verses 17 and 18, David reflects again on God's infinite knowledge. David is included in all of God's thoughts; God is with him until the end. God's thoughts cannot be counted. God's knowledge cannot be measured. When we think with the mind of God, we can begin to think outside the box and focus on the awesomeness of God within us. As our enslaved ancestors did, African Americans can envision ways to fulfill their full potential outside of set social boundaries. Furthermore, David's lament reaches out to everyone in that it tears down boundaries based on race, gender, and class. It defines each of us as living in the mind of God. Seeing the world through David's theological perspective, people can fully participate in a relationship with God and each other.

## *You Can Run But You Cannot Hide: Psalm 139:7-12*

The attribute of God that says that God is everywhere at the same time makes God omnipresent. This is this characteristic that the psalmist speaks of in 139:7. He asks a rhetorical question, "Where can I go from your spirit or where can I flee from your presence?" David is not seeking a literal answer here. He asks this question to illustrate how great the expanse of God's being and God's spirit is. David suggests that God's spirit is inescapable. This must have been a comforting fact for enslaved Africans estranged from their homeland who found the courage to trust in an unseen God who would one day deliver them from the bondage of slavery. This God would first free their minds and spirits to rejoice and celebrate the great love, peace, and mercy that God offered through Jesus Christ.

God was and is omnipresent, ever present, everywhere at the same time, always with us in our past, our present as well as our future. God is also omnipotent which means that God is all-powerful. Like our ancestors, we can cast our cares on God and rest in knowing that indeed the Creator is all-powerful and will provide solutions to our problems because God cares for each of us. And because God is omniscient, there is nothing that God does not know about us. However, this fact is often troublesome for some contemporary Christians seeking to hide from God's inescapable spirit in an attempt to live in denial and to camouflage their sin. Christians today sometimes keep God at arms length while wondering where is God in the time of need or trouble. The psalmist advances this idea by saying in verses 4-5, "Even before a word is on my tongue, O LORD you know it completely. You hem me in, behind and before, and lay your hand upon me." This however is considered by the psalmist to be a wonderful thing. He says, "Such knowledge is too wonderful for me; it is so high that I cannot attain it (v. 6), another way of saying, "He's so high you can't get over him."

Though we may sometimes stray away from God, God never strays from us. You can run but you cannot hide from God. There is nowhere on earth or in heaven where one can ever escape the presence of God. Though we may even turn our backs on God, God never turns away from us. Though we cannot see God with the naked eye, God sees us, and we can see the result of God's presence and God's works all around us. God's presence is always available to us.

Psalm 139 stresses the idea of the ever-present nature of God. Verses 8-10 illuminate this idea, "If I ascend to heaven you are there; if I make my bed in Sheol, you are there. If I take the wings of the morning and settle at the farthest limits of the sea, even there your hand shall lead me, and your right hand shall hold me fast." God's presence is perpetual and steadfast. In all that we do or say God is there. Even from our conception God was there planting in our DNA the seeds of all that we would need for our lives, as the Rev. James Forbes of the Riverside Church in New York City says. God's master plan and blueprint for each of us was laid from the beginning of our lives.

God is present in our times of joy and sorrow, our periods of trial and triumph as well as our moments of laughter and tears. Accessing God is as easy as calling a friend on the telephone. God's support and nurture are always just a prayer away and often, even before we ask, God is right there.

**Even if we are forced to make our beds in hell still nothing can separate us from God's love.**

When we suffer we are often asked by critics of the faith just as David was asked and as Christ was asked, "Where is your God"? (Psalm 42:3) Jesus himself pleaded in desperation and in his own humanity, "My God, my God, why have you forsaken me?" (Matthew 27:46; Psalm 22:1). It appeared at the time that God had left Jesus to suffer alone on the cross along with the two thieves who hung beside him. But in actuality we never go through any situation alone. God was there with Jesus as he faced the most difficult task of his calling, suffering and death on the cross; likewise, God is with us in our trials. For God is a participant in our pain and suffering. It has often been suggested that at the most difficult times in our lives God picks us up and carries us.

As the apostle Paul taught, nothing can separate us from the love of God through Jesus Christ. He said, "For I am convinced that neither death, nor life, nor angels, nor rulers, nor things present, nor things to come, nor powers, nor height, nor depth, nor anything else in all creation, will be able to separate us from the love of God in Christ Jesus our Lord" (Romans 8:37-39). Even if we were forced to make our beds in hell, as David proclaimed, still nothing can separate us from God's love. Not even death can break the bond of love that flows from God to God's people. Even in death God is with us.

## *A Most Excellent Psalm, A Most Excellent Song*

David's Psalm 139 has been called a "most excellent psalm" by biblical scholars because it gives the reader a glimpse of the wonder and awesome nature of God. It is pure praise at its best. It is a psalm of trust and adoration, the personal prayer of the psalmist whose awe of God is splendidly articulated. Though our finite minds will never be able to fully comprehend the totality of the being that is God, the psalmist gives us a beautiful glimpse of the attributes of God. Perhaps this is why God's grace abounds. God sees our weaknesses and our frailties and graciously looks beyond our faults to speak to our needs.

David prays to the Lord in this psalm as if he is well aware of his insignificance in comparison to God's greatness. David speaks in awesome wonder of God's wisdom, God's nurture, and God's love saying, you've searched me, you've known me, you've formed me, and you've kept me.

His love and gratitude touch the heart with tenderness as his lament gives way to inspired praise. That praise also flows from this beloved spiritual, "My God Is So High," whether sung from the skillful voice of opera singer Kathleen Battle, the sweet innocent shouts of a children's choir, or in the haunting voices of ancestors deep in the hush arbor.

## Food for Thought

1. *This spiritual says that God's being is at once high, low, and wide. What does this mean in relation to you as an individual Christian?*

2. *How does your faith sustain you in times of trouble? What Scripture or Scriptures remind you of the sustaining power of faith?*

3. *What elements of the 139th Psalm make it a "most excellent psalm" to you? In what ways can this psalm be empowering to you? What other psalms do you find empowering?*

4. *What do you know about the hush arbor or the "invisible church"? What is its importance to the Black Church today?*

# Lesson 2
# Joshua Fit de Battle of Jericho

Joshua 6:8 -11, 14b-16

**Key Verse**
Joshua said to the people, "Shout for the LORD has given you the city."
(Joshua 6:16b)

**Theme**
Celebrate a faith that gives us determination to reach goals.

**Proverb**
Slowly, slowly the porridge goes into the gourd.
Kenya, Tanzania

**Word**
Determination

***"Joshua Fit de Battle of Jericho"***
**Chorus**

Joshua fit de battle of Jericho, Jericho, Jericho
Joshua fit de battle of Jericho
And the walls came tumbelin' down

**Verse**

You may talk about your King Gideon
You may talk about your man of Saul
There's none like good ole Joshua
At de battle of Jericho

**Verse**

Up to the walls of Jericho
He marched with spear in hand
Go blow them ram horns Joshua cried
'Cause the battle am in my hand.

## *Let's Listen: A Song of Victory*

In the churches and services sponsored by "Christian" masters, the slaves often heard sermons admonishing them to be obedient and not steal. The hush arbor is where the slaves learned the biblical stories of freedom, of God's intervention in the affairs of humankind. The story about Joshua and the walls of Jericho is one that models faith and obedience to God. It is also a story in which the weak win out over the strong; an army of nomads comes from the wilderness and destroys a fortified city with only trumpets and a great deal of walking and yelling. The Bible tells how Joshua's army walked around the walled city of Jericho once a day for six days. Each time they walked, the priests blew trumpets. On the seventh day they circled the city seven times, blew the horns and shouted, and the walls of the city came crashing down.

What a story about which to create a song! Even as they lived mostly in rural areas, the institution of slavery represented an incredibly fortified city to those in bondage. Yet they sang that "the walls came tumbelin' down." They rehearsed the story of a newly freed, homeless people in a lively melody. With rhythmic repetition, they emphasized the strength of Jericho's walls, utilizing words as a battering ram to break down in their spirits and minds the oppressive effects of living an enslaved existence. This energetic song of victory and community lifted their spirits to a hope that the walls that surrounded them could come down; freedom could be won. God is faithful. God made a way for the Hebrew children to experience victory and God will make a way for them.

> **"Once my maw and paw taken me and Katherine after night to slip to 'nother place to a prayin'- and singin' . . . We prays for the end of trib'lation and the end of beatin's and for shoes that fit our feet."**
>
> **(Mary Reynolds, ex-slave)**

## *Marching Around the City: Joshua 6:8-16*

The battle of Jericho is about hope and determination. It is about faith and obedience to bring about change. After more than four hundred years of slavery and forty years of battling the challenges of the wilderness, those who were with Joshua were determined to make it to the Promised Land.

Forty years passed before the Israelites would make it to see that great day when the walls of Jericho would fall. When Jericho was first scouted out, twelve men went to survey the territory. Ten men came back reporting that surely it would be impossible for their modest band of warriors to defeat the giants who dwelled in this mighty city. Only Joshua and Caleb believed the contrary. Though they agreed that it might not be an easy task, with the help of God, who got them out of bondage in Egypt, they had confidence that the Israelites could prevail over Jericho. The people, however, had forgotten the many miracles that the Lord had performed for them, such as parting the Red Sea, drowning Pharaoh's army so that they could make their mass exodus, or sending manna from heaven when they were hungry in the desert. Because of this, God waited until all of the original people who came out of Egypt, except Joshua and Caleb, died before bringing them to the Promised Land. Before entering the city, the Israelites led by the priests had to do something radical—march, play music, and shout.

At first the Israelites marched in silence. They remained silent for six days, patiently marching around the city without speaking a word as they had been instructed to do. The armed men went first and the seven priests with seven ram horns followed. This was an act of faith and obedience on their part as they marched.

On the seventh day, they marched around the city seven times. At the seventh lap, Joshua instructed all of the people to "Shout, for the Lord has given you the city!" (v. 16b) With that shout, the rugged stone-based walls, eleven feet high, topped with thirty-five feet of smooth stone, collapsed. They "came tumbelin' down" as the spiritual says. The Israelites were able to go in and lay claim to their Promised Land of Canaan. They victoriously shouted and blew their trumpets in celebration of the land that God had given to them.

## A New Promised Land

The African American story of liberation has parallels in this story. Marching and shouting are not uncommon in African American faith communities. The Civil Rights Movement of the 1960's, largely made up of Black Church parishioners, found thousands of supportive people of every ethnic persuasion and religious creed uniting in moral conscience to march around the cities of the South and in the North, where racial segregation and discrimination had become the norm. Symbolically they, too, received their marching orders from on high as they discerned the perfect will of God as interpreted and articulated through leaders like Martin Luther King, Jr., Wyatt Tee Walker, Joseph Lowry and James Lawson. They marched to bring down the walls of racial discrimination and segregation. They marched without arms in the spirit of nonviolent protest. They often sang while they marched, lifting up songs of protest as well as old African American spirituals. They shouted in worship services, then and now, in thanksgiving for all that God had done for them in spite of their circumstances.

When European settlers came to America, they held the notion that

America was their promised land and that they were the new "chosen people." They even espoused a kind of civil religion that was at the heart of the endeavors of the founders. They combined mottos, such as "In God We Trust" and "God Bless America," with the politics of founding a new nation as evidence of their sense of God's favor. Unfortunately the settlers built this new nation on the backs of enslaved Africans stolen from their homeland. This legacy took the country through slavery, freedom, and the Jim Crow era. African Americans, tired of being left out of the bountiful blessings enjoyed by their white counterparts, decided to outwardly respond to the inner voice of protest to tear down the walls of injustice, prejudice, and discrimination. They too sought their promised land.

During the 1980's South Africans also sang, danced, and marched their way to freedom from apartheid (uh-part-hite). Nelson Mandela, Bishop Desmond Tutu and many others were willing to take actions that helped to tear down structures that prevented abundant life for black South Africans. By collective work and responsibility (Ujima, one of the Kwanzaa principles), the walls can come down in any situation. Had the Joshua story taken place in the twenty-first century, someone would have suggested hiring a demolition squad to knock the walls down. However, Joshua followed God's instructions and marched.

There have been many leaders who have led African Americans to bring down walls, including Fannie Lou Hamer, Charles Houston, and Thurgood Marshall. They sought to bring down the walls of mis-education, disenfranchisement, and segregation in order to build up the community.

**The African American story of liberation has parallels in the Joshua story.**

## *Keep Marching*

African Americans have a long way to go before reaching an ideal promised land. Our churches must continue to resist practices and structures that cripple our communities. We must be willing to keep vigils, break down walls, and speak out. A determination to fulfill the vision to better the condition of the African American community and indeed all of God's people lies in understanding that "Slowly, slowly the porridge goes into the gourd." (Kenya)

Education and economic development are two major keys to the kingdom that still elude many people of color. Education is one of the best ways for people to better themselves individually and collectively.

Education not only expands the mind but also increases opportunities for career development. Our churches would do well to partner with our schools to assist youth in obtaining the best possible education, leading them toward college entrance.

Economically many churches encourage tithing programs, but they should also encourage savings programs, helping youth and adults understand and appreciate the regularity of tithing and saving in order to build a strong economic and spiritual base for the future. Many churches have health and wellness ministries, and others would do well to follow suit.

Numerous problems still impede the success of people of color and poor people of all races, young and old in America. Unemployment, homelessness, incarceration, poverty, racism, sexism, ageism, AIDS, cancer, high blood pressure, diabetes and teen pregnancy are among the many problems people face today. Many are turning to the church to seek help in conquering some of these problems.

When those who were enslaved sang "Joshua Fit de Battle of Jericho," perhaps they were able to envision a future where the walls of slavery and injustice would someday tumble down. While they sang this biblically based song of liberation, it could secure a hope for their future and for the future of their offspring. Surely they believed that one day the walls of slavery would indeed crumble and they would be free. And as those offspring would see that dream come to fruition, their offspring, too, could also sing the same spiritual and envision a world of equality, justice, and tolerance. So they lifted their voices in a holy shout in the thick brush of the hush arbor, where their shouts could be hidden from the ears of their oppressors, but valiantly raised to the ears of their God who would hear their cry and "answer by and by."

## *Food for Thought*

1. *What was the purpose of daily marching around the city of Jericho?*
2. *The Civil Rights Era of the 1960's stressed nonviolent protest methods such as peaceful marches, sit-ins, and boycotts in order to gain justice and equality. The biblical story of Joshua however is a story of war. Here the people march into battle to win the Promised Land. How do these two extremes from contemporary history and biblical history impact upon current affairs such as the war in Iraq?*
3. *Though African Americans were freed from slavery, they were not liberated from social problems such as, homelessness, unemployment and incarceration. How does the Word of God offer liberation? What is your vision for God's people regarding freedom, liberation, and empowerment?*

# Lesson 3

# Little David, Play on Your Harp

I Samuel 16:14-23

**Key Verse**

"David took the lyre and played it with his hand,
and Saul would be relieved and feel better." (I Samuel 16:23)

**Theme**

Celebrate faith in a God who can give peace.

**Proverb**

After hardship comes relief.

**Word**

Peace

***"Little David, Play on Your Harp"***

**Chorus**

Little David, play on your harp, Hallelu, Hallelu
Little David, play on your harp, Hallelu,

**Verse**

Little David was a shepherd boy,
He killed Goliath and shouted for joy

**Verse**

Joshua was the son of Nun
He never would quit, 'til his work was done

## *Let's Listen: A Playful Song*

A light-hearted spiritual with a playful, upbeat pace, "Little David Play on Your Harp" is another example of the Bible teaching and learning that occurred in the worship and lives of enslaved Africans. Undoubtedly it lifted the spirits of the ancestors and generations after who sang it. Indeed, one could easily listen to this melody that is now usually relegated to children's repertoire and get the impression that the slaves must have been happy because they were singing. Such a joyful tune can only bring a smile to the face and skip to the step and a bounce to the head. The story behind the song, however, is one of defiance and torment. Even so it is a fitting example of how the music that came out of oppressive circumstances took some of the sting out of suffering.

From Africa to Israel to Greece to slavery in America, music has been used therapeutically. The process of creating African American spirituals was a type of music therapy. Music in the slave community provided healing and release for people whose very humanity was being suffocated by oppression and cruelty. They needed to be where they could "sing all de way through, an' hum 'long, an' shout, jist turn loose lak." The development of the spiritual in wilderness places shows how God's spirit works through the creative abilities of a people to produce not only a new art form, but a form of healing.

Music can indeed affect the mood. Music therapists use music in assisting patients to feel better and ease anxiety while psychiatrists discourage patients suffering from depression from listening to sad music as it can further depress the patient. Music Therapy is a discipline that is especially geared toward helping people with emotional, physical, and psychological problems find healing and joy.

Music therapist Celeste K. Brooks has worked with patients in nursing homes in Washington, D.C. for almost twenty years. Her clients are victims of dementia, Alzheimer's, stroke, and Chronic Brain Syndrome (associated with alcohol abuse). In talking about a thirty-eight-year-old client whose brain and personality had been damaged by a stroke at the age of sixteen, she relates, "With the music we sang together, [this client] was able to lay down some of her troubles long enough to communicate her deepest feelings. We were able to share those thoughts with the staff that worked directly with her and life became just a little more peaceful. She also became more outgoing."

Mabel Thornton tells a story about her father, Rev. Isaiah Wilkinson, who had pastored in rural Virginia from 1915 to 1949. After some debilitating illnesses, his mind became cloudy. He did not know people and became nonresponsive. One day another minister came to visit him. Family members told him that their father would not recognize him or respond in any way. The visiting minister simply began to sing "Amazing Grace." With a strong voice Rev. Wilkinson joined in, singing every verse. Music engages the deepest parts of the brain, the body, and the spirit.

## *An Evil Spirit From the Lord: I Samuel 16:14-16*

The African proverb says, "After hardship comes relief." Sometimes that relief comes a bit faster when there is music to soothe the ailing spirit. Such was the case with Saul who had been tormented by an evil spirit. The spirit of God had left Saul and an evil spirit had taken up residence in God's place. Samuel had been the spiritual leader of the Israelites. However, the people decided that they wanted a king rather than a spiritual leader. Samuel warned that there would be problems the people had not considered if they established new leadership. But they decided that since other nations had a king, they should as well. God led Samuel to Saul and told him that Saul would be king over the people.

> **"On Sundays, us would git tergether in de woods an' have worship. Us could go to de white folks' church, but us wanted ter go whar us could sing all de way through, an' hum 'long, an' shout— yo' all know, jist turn' loose lak."**
> **(Emily Dixon, ex-slave)**

Then the spirit of God took control of Saul and stayed with him until Saul disobeyed his orders to conquer the Amalekites (I Samuel 15). Instead, Saul spared them because they had favored him in the past. Saul kept their livestock for his own kingdom. His disobedience led to punishment—God's spirit departed from him. According to the Bible, God even sent an evil spirit that would periodically terrorize Saul. What was said in biblical times to be of evil spirits might be interpreted in modern times to be a sign of mental illness, such as depression or paranoia. Saul was given to extremely violent acts at times (I Samuel 18:8-11) and would eventually massacre his entire priesthood (I Samuel 22).

Some may find it problematic that the evil spirit is said to have come from God. When Job suffered at the hands of the devil, he reasoned that God gives and God takes away (Job 1:21). "Shall we receive the good at the hand of God, and not receive the bad?" (2:10) He blessed God as the originator of everything, the good and the bad. Early Christianity makes a shift in this way of thinking. In 1 John 4:1-2, the writer cautions, "Beloved, do not believe every spirit, but test the spirits to see whether they are from God . . . every spirit that confesses that Jesus Christ has come in the flesh is from God." From the cultural context of the ancient world, the Hebrew Bible reports that Saul's depression is caused by a spirit from God. And indeed whenever we do the things that separate us from the will of God, we can expect to suffer. We were created to be in communion with God and a breach in our relationship with our Creator will cause dis-ease and a lack of peace. All mental illness, however, does not necessarily have a spiritual root. A malfunctioning bio-chemical system in the body can also cause dis-ease of the mind.

In Africa, persons play upon the *mbira* (a.k.a. sansa, kalimba, thumb piano) to settle the mind before going to sleep. African Americans created the spiritual to soothe their souls in the midst of slavery. In like fashion, Saul's servants suggest to him music, specifically stringed music, to ease his suffering. Through Psalms especially, biblical readers recognize the value in giving God praise. When people give a sacrifice of praise, there is a release of suffering and an outpouring of God's peace and comfort. When the servants offer to find Saul a musician, they are really suggesting him to get his praise on. The role of music in this instance is to release the influence of the evil spirit on Saul.

> **We were created to be in communion with God, and a breach in our relationship with our Creator will cause dis-ease.**

## *The Peoples' Choice or God's Choice*

Both Saul and his servants want a skilled musician. In presenting David, they emphasize his musical skills along with his character and his relationship with God. In order for Saul to experience a spiritual relief, the music had to be delivered by one who had a spiritual relationship with God. He sent for David to come to him and play on his lyre, a type of hand-held harp. David played the lyre so beautifully that some believed his music almost had magical power. David's playing caused the evil spirit to leave Saul. It was chased away by this sweet music that brought peace and stillness to his tormented soul. Every time David played his harp, the evil spirit left Saul, and he felt peace and comfort. Saul developed a fondness for David. He liked him so much that he requested that David might come and live with him.

Saul, however, was completely unaware that God had decided to choose a new king because of Saul's defiance of God's orders. That king would be the young David. Though David, the youngest son of Jesse, grew to be a fierce and brave warrior and a great king chosen by God to succeed Saul, he was well known as a skilled musician. He was the only person willing to take on the mighty nine-foot tall giant Goliath, a warrior for the Philistines who were terrorizing the Israelites (I Samuel 17).

The first verse of "Little David" gives a short biography of David and a summary of the Goliath story. It tells us that David was a shepherd who killed Goliath and shouted for joy! The Bible tells us that, "When David returned from killing the Philistine, women came out of all the towns . . . singing and dancing . . . with songs of joy." The lyrics of their songs went like this:

> "Saul has killed his thousands,
> and David his ten thousands." (I Samuel 17:6-8)

Saul was not happy with this turn of events and from this time forward began to persecute David.

## Singing Through a Storm

Enslaved Africans endured immense hardship and persecution while victims of chattel slavery. Singing the spirituals aided them in dealing with their circumstances, guiding them through the storms of their lives. Since many were unable to read and those who could read were forbidden to do so, they learned countless Bible stories through singing about them. A good example is that of the life of King David. Their theology was shaped through singing songs of hope and empowerment that came from the Bible. The singing of this music allowed their spirits to be lifted out of the depths of despair and often served as a vehicle for the expression of painful emotions locked in their spirits as a result of atrocities of slavery. This music resonated with their circumstances and gave them hope for the future.

Civil Rights leader and pastor Wyatt Tee Walker studied the evolution of the music of the black religious experience from slavery to contemporary times. In his book *"somebody's CALLING my name": black sacred music and SOCIAL CHANGE*, he outlines this evolution in something he called the music tree which traces its development from spirituals, gospel, jazz, and rhythm and blues. He believed all of this music grew out of the early singing done by those in slavery. Some of the music told stories of their suffering and the harsh treatment they endured. He noted, "If you look at what Black people are singing, it will provide a clue as to what is happening to them sociologically."

> **"If you look at what Black people are singing, it will provide a clue as to what is happening to them sociologically."**
> **(Wyatt Tee Walker)**

Rabbi Moshe Kwalbrun, a Jewish teacher of forty years who grew up in a Black neighborhood in Brooklyn, New York, also echoes these sentiments. He recalls hearing the spirituals sung and the haunting soul inspiring effect it had on him. Songs like "Go Down Moses," he says, were particularly inspiring. He also recalls with admiration seeing the relatively poor blacks in the neighborhood dress up in their finest clothes, little girls in ruffled dresses and patent leather shoes going to worship on Sunday mornings. Though they faced difficulty during the week, Sunday was a time for worship, praise, and singing at the local church.

The same was true for those worshipping in the hush arbor. Deep in the thick brush of quiet woods they could cry out to God about all that they were going through. Here was a place and a time where they could bring their troubles to God and believe that their prayers would be heard. The spiritual "Lord, How Cum Me Here?" illustrates this idea. It is a song of a young mother sung in the form of a prayer that asks God why am I here in this predicament. She says, "They sold my chillen' away. There ain't no freedom here. They treat me so mean here, Lord; I wish I never was born," as she echoes the sentiments of the suffering servant Job. Songs like this were sung in response to atrocities that those who were enslaved endured.

## *Enduring the Suffering*

Consider the story told by Julia Foot, an itinerant black female preacher. Her younger sister resisted the advances of her slave master. She confided in her mistress concerning the matter. Instead of coming to her aid, she was beaten. The mistress ordered her wounds washed with salt water and then had her dressed in a rough cotton dress that stuck fast to the fresh open wounds. When the younger sister was unable to remove her dress because the fabric stuck to her back, it was cruelly yanked from her by the slave master's wife. Along with the dress came new scabs and her agony began all over again.

Similar stories can be found in other slave narratives. Such suffering reminds us of Jesus on the cross. Those who endured slavery and those who are still oppressed today can view Christ as a participant in their suffering. This notion of an enduring and steadfast Savior who is ever-present has allowed Christians then and now to be jubilant even in suffering and has essentially fostered a kind of spiritual genius in black religious folk. While singing by no means indicates happiness or being happy-go-lucky, music provides a vehicle that enables the community to find peace in the midst of evil and gives the strength to overcome. Our music, no matter the style, must continue to be therapeutic, designed to help individuals find comfort, joy, healing, and salvation in God.

*Julia Foote's spiritual autobiography is included in the book "Spiritual Narratives, the Schomburg Library of Nineteenth-Century Black Woman Writers."

## *Food for Thought*

1. *What songs provide relief for your suffering when you are going through difficult times?*

2. *What is it about the music birthed out of slavery and the music of the black religious experience that sustains people through trouble and strife?*

3. *Compare the passion and suffering of Christ with the atrocities of slavery and tragic events in modern history. What parallels do you see regarding the human response to suffering across time?*

# Lesson 4

# De Blind Man

Luke 18:35-43

**Key Verse**
Jesus said to him, "Receive your sight; your faith has saved you."
(Luke 18:42)

**Theme**
Celebrate a faith that leads to salvation.

**African Proverb**
God provides for the blind vulture. (Mali, Senegal, Niger)

**Word**
Faith

***"De Blind Man"***
**Verse**
Oh de blind man stood on the road and cried
Oh de blind man stood on the road and cried
**Chorus**
Cryin', "Oh, my Lord, save me!"
De blind man stood on the road and cried.
**Verse**
Cryin' dat he might receive his sight
Cryin' dat he might receive his sight
**Verse**
Cryin', "What kind of shoes am dose you wear?"
Cryin', "What kind of shoes am dose you wear?"
**Verse**
Cryin', "Dese shoes I wear am de gospel shoes."
Cryin', "Dese shoes I wear am de gospel shoes."

## *Let's Listen: A Song of Petition*

This spiritual tells the story of a blind man whose faith in Christ resulted in a restoration of sight. This song has a melancholy mood that concentrates on the blind man's petitions to the man called Jesus. It begins with a simple statement of the situation. Except for the bluesy half-step tones on "road and," the melody is fairly unremarkable. The emphasis is on the story being told. "Oh de blind man stood on the road and cried." This is repeated, without the blues tones, five steps higher. It is as if the creators of the song just wanted to make sure that we understand the setting.

The next phrase informs us of the content of the blind man's cries. He is asking for salvation. Here the melodic line reaches its highest pitch to elicit an emotional response to a plea that pierces the heart, "Ooooooh, my Lord! Save me!" And yet there appears to be no doubt or hesitation in the petition. The blind man is addressing one with whom he is spiritually acquainted; he says "My Lord!" And then he says, "Save me." The slave creators of this song no doubt knew that Jesus was true to his name, Jesus, meaning "He saves." By mouthing the words of the blind man they indeed made their own plea. "My Lord, save me!" Save us from sin! Save us from death! Save us from spiritual blindness! Save us from slavery! Save us from oppression! We should continue to sing this song offering a singular petition, save us, Lord!

## *The Road to Jericho: Luke 18:35-39*

The road between Jerusalem and Jericho was a well-traveled road. The story of the Good Samaritan gives us an idea of its usage (Luke 10:30). It was on this road that a traveler was attacked by robbers, ignored by a Levite and a priest, and eventually cared for by a Samaritan. The blind man no doubt had the opportunity to earn more money on this road than another less traveled one. Likewise poor persons who solicit on the street in modern society do so in strategic places, where people travel frequently and are likely to have spare change to give. In biblical times there was no opportunity for a blind person to make a living other than to be a beggar on the street. On this day, however, one very special traveler passed by. It was Jesus. The blind man quickly seized his opportunity to gain a miracle. Though he was physically blind, spiritually he was sighted for he recognized a great opportunity to have his life changed.

The blind man called Jesus the Son of David. Perhaps he believed that Jesus was the Messiah with the power to save the people from all that ailed them. He quickly seized the opportunity to ask for what he wanted and sorely needed. Jesus said, "Ask, and it will be given; search, and you will find; knock, and the door will be opened for you" (Matthew 7:7). Often, however, people go to the Lord with a shopping list of requests for things that they desire, rather than the things they actually need. At the same time the Bible warns, "You do not have because you do not ask. You ask and do not receive because you ask wrongly in order to spend what you get on your pleasures" (James 4:3). The blind man asked for what he truly needed as well as desired. When the others tried to silence him, he shouted even louder asking Jesus to have mercy on him. It rattled the people's nerves because as far as they were concerned, the man had no right to shout — he was a beggar, poor, disabled, outcast. No one, however, could stop him from seizing the opportunity to receive his sight!

**"Marster neber 'low he slaves to go to chu'ch. Dey hab big holes out in de fiel's dey git down in and pray. Dey done dat way' cause de white folks didn't want 'em to pray. Dey uster pray for freedom."**
**(Ellen Butler, ex-slave)**

Believers in the slave community were also shunted to the side. If allowed to worship with the rest of the church community, it was in galleries, in the back, or standing on the side. Out in the wilderness, black Christians could have "real" worship. Despite their disabled, outcast position in society, in the hush arbor they could focus on the realization that Jesus was one who came to give sight to the blind and to release the prisoners. "And why not every man?" Our churches must be a place where people are free to ask for what they need.

## *Faith and Action: Luke 18:40-43*

Some people are so intimidated by the challenges of life that they give up on themselves and God. They become comfortable in an environment that has been manipulated to help them function. What motivates the blind man? Faith. When the blind man calls out to Jesus, he refers to him as the "Son of David." In acknowledging who Jesus is, he demonstrates his faith in what Jesus can do. His spiritual vision was

20/20. Perhaps he realized that "God provides [even] for the blind vulture." Unlike the rich young ruler (18:18-30), the blind man could feel his need for restoration to the community. Only sight could facilitate this. After having the blind man brought to him, Jesus asks, "What can I do for you?" Jesus requires him to participate in his healing process by getting him to focus on what he wants. The blind man just does not want to see, he wants to see "again." Unlike the man who was born blind in John 9, this man, called Bartimaeus in Mark 10:46, had previously been able to see. He'd had vision at one time and somehow lost it. Yet he had faith enough to ask.

In the ancient world, blindness and diseases of the eye were common illnesses. A frequent eye disease in Palestine and Egypt was *ophthalmia* (off-**thal**-mee-yuh), an inflammation of the connecting tissue of the eye. It was characterized by an oozing discharge. Caused by flies that landed on a sleeping infant's eyes at night, it sometimes resulted in permanent blindness. All disease was attributed to sin. Affected persons found themselves excluded from the mainstream of community, begging to survive. Even his position on the side of the road to Jericho points to the blind man's sidelined position in society. Nevertheless, confidently though desperately, he called out to Jesus, as if he instinctively knew that Jesus would be both willing and able to heal his infirmity.

With the blind man Jesus shows that healing requires both faith and action. Jesus said to the man, "Receive your sight; your faith has saved you." Jesus suggests that the man's own efforts, crying out to the Lord in faith, caused a miraculous change in his circumstance. Jesus said the same of the woman with an issue of blood who announced if she could merely touch his garment she would be healed. Jesus told the woman, "Daughter, your faith has made you well." (Mark 5:34) Yet, the miracles that Jesus performed while he walked the earth served to glorify God. People began to believe in Jesus as the Messiah and in so doing Jesus rewarded those who exhibited great faith as the blind man did.

**"We used to steal off to de woods and have church, like de spirit moved us–sing and pray to our own liking and soul satisfaction."**

**(Susan Rhodes, ex-slave)**

Human beings need a constant renewing of vision and faith. Without vision, the people perish (Proverbs 29:18). Often people start out with a vision and then they are faced with the blinders of life—negative thinking, stress, financial hardship, tragedy, and so on. They lose their vision and end up in a begging position. However, the rekindling of faith can restore spiritual sight. When the blind man received his sight (18:43), the crowd's criticism turned into praise. His disability had excluded him from community. Jesus Christ used his faith to restore his sight and his place in community.

## *Music That Ministers*

The spirituals served to provide enslaved Africans with comfort and support in dire circumstances. Some of the music also served as a source of joy. Here they could sing their troubles away. Still other times the music served as a vehicle for communicating messages such as "Steal Away to Jesus." This song may have announced an escape attempt, or it might have alerted the people that it was time to steal away to the hush arbor for a camp meeting. There the people could come and have their spirits ministered to through singing songs that seemed to have come down from heaven to take them through the toils of life in slavery.

The spirituals ministered to the slaves by providing, hope, determination, and a sense of well-being. They still have the capacity to minister to the human spirit today. Louvinia Pointer, a retired music teacher, is the director of the Great Day Chorale in Brooklyn, N.Y. She has taken her chorale behind bars to sing songs like, "De Blind Man," "Joshua Fit de Battle," "My God Is So High," "Lord, How Cum Me Here?" and many others. She has found receptive audiences in the young incarcerated men and women whose hearts receive the music as a welcoming comfort to their souls. She tells her audiences that the spiritual gives us a glimpse into the souls of the slaves. She continues to share this music because she believes that although black Americans are no longer chained physically, there are many problems of life that still bind them. For her, spirituals

**Human beings need a constant renewing of vision and faith. Without vision, the people perish.**

provides hope, determination and a sense well-being.

Spirituals and songs based on spirituals were sung to deepen the faith of those fighting for Civil Rights in America during the sixties. This movement inspired South Africans in their quest for justice. Nelson Mandela was incarcerated for 27 years and forced to work in a rock quarry where the daily pounding of rock caused the irritating dust to settle in his eyes. His eyes were badly damaged after so many years of working in the quarry. Nevertheless, though the oppression continued behind bars, the quest for redemption and righteousness continued. Mandela's quest for deliverance from apartheid (uh-part-hite) was relentless. He had faith enough to ask for what he and his people deserved. He asked God to deliver them. He asked the people to strive toward freedom and never lose hope. He admonished those who were incarcerated with him to keep their eyes on the prize. He petitioned the government to stand up and do what was right and dismantle apartheid. He was willing to sacrifice his freedom, his eyesight, and even his life for that which was right!

South Africans utilized music and dance to lift their spirits and make them strong in the long fight for freedom. Singing in community promotes solidarity, a feeling of togetherness, that we are not alone. Singing builds up faith and facilitates miracles. Paul and Silas were praying and singing in prison when an earthquake from God shook the foundations and opened the prison doors (Acts 16:25-33). Paul and Silas did not try to escape but sought the salvation of the jailer. Let us keep singing, "Oh my Lord, save me!" until the foundations of physical and spiritual oppression can no longer bind or blind.

## Food for Thought

1. *Why did the people on the street wish to silence the blind man? Did they believe he was not worthy of healing?*

2. *Is healing a reward for faith, a demonstration of the power given to the blind man from God or both?*

3. *Did Jesus perform miracles of healing for the benefit of believers, nonbelievers or both?*

4. *How does music minister to us? Why does music reach us when the spoken word sometimes cannot?*

# Lesson 5

# Come Out de Wilderness

Luke 15:1-7

**Key Verse**

Rejoice with me for I have found my sheep that was lost. (Luke 15:6)

**Theme**

Celebrate the joy of salvation in Jesus Christ.

**African Proverb**

If you do not rejoice when a friend gets nine, you yourself will never get ten. (Ghana)

**Word**

Joy

***"Come Out de Wilderness"***

Tell me, how did you feel when you come out de wilderness,
Come out de wilderness, come out de wilderness
Tell me, how did you feel when you come out de wilderness
Leaning on de Lord

Well, I loved ev'rybody when I come out de wilderness
Come out de wilderness, come out de wilderness
I loved ev'rybody when I come out de wilderness
Leaning on de Lord

Well, my soul was so happy when I come out de wilderness,
Come out de wilderness, come out de wilderness
My soul was so happy when I come out de wilderness,
Leaning on de Lord

## *Let's Listen: A Song of Celebration*

This jubilant song of celebration and salvation, "Come out de Wilderness" asks listeners not to take their feelings for granted but to stop and examine them. It exuberantly asks in call and response fashion, "How did it feel when you came out of the wilderness?" It says, "Give me a description of what you felt when you found the Lord, or when you finally gained your freedom, or in the case of a runaway like Denmark Vesey (see Introduction) when you came out of hiding." Surely in the first two cases, it was a day of rejoicing. In each and every case it was still an occasion to continue to lean upon the Lord. Though the newly freed would have nothing more to look forward to in their immediate future but hunger, poverty, homelessness, and imprisonment, still that initial jolt of liberation had to be an exhilarating one. This song encouraged them to take note of it, to talk about it, sing about it, celebrate it, rejoice in it, and most of all, remember to lean on God!

The song leader switches person in the next two verses. In the first verse she asks the question. Now she answers the question. She responds by telling how she felt when she came out of the wilderness. First of all, she loved everybody! Out there in the wilderness she had an encounter with the God of love and it caused her to love everybody. No exceptions are made, whether slave or free, black or white, male or female (Galatians 3:28); she loves everybody! Another outcome of her travail in the wilderness is joy. Her soul is so happy. Something happened in those woods that brought joy and a peace that passed all understanding (Philippians 4:4-7). In order to continue in this spirit of love and joy, she must trust God and depend on Jesus Christ.

## *A Story: Luke 15:1-7*

The foundation for this spiritual can be found in Luke 15. It begins with the criticism of Jesus by the Pharisees that he is spending time with tax collectors and sinners rather than the so-called righteous folk—them. The Pharisees were a sect of Jews who prided themselves on knowing and keeping the Law of Moses. Unlike modern times where those who don't pay their taxes are scorned and face imprisonment, in biblical times tax collectors, also known as publicans, were called sinners. They were considered as traitors because they were Jews who unfairly overburdened other Jews with taxes, asking for even more than the Roman government required and then keeping the difference. No respectable Jewish person, and certainly not a Pharisee, would take time with tax collectors, but here Jesus was offering the gospel to them.

The Pharisees criticized him and asked why he would do such a thing. Even as Nicodemus (John 3:1-21) and Joseph of Arimathea

(Mark 15:42-47) were both Pharisees, Jesus accused the Pharisees as a group to be rather self-righteous and hypocritical (Matthew 23:13-36). They always wanted to know why Jesus did the things he did. They wanted to know why he performed healings and other miraculous works on the Sabbath. But Jesus only replied, "My father is still working and I also am working" (John 5:17).

Rather than respond to the Pharisees' accusations of why he was talking to the traitorous tax collectors, he told them the parable of the lost sheep. He asked, "Which one of you, having a hundred sheep and losing one of them does not leave the ninety in the wilderness and go after the one that is lost" (v. 4). In the time of Christ a herd of one hundred sheep was a very large herd. No shepherd would think of leaving even one sheep behind. Jesus went on to say that the shepherd called all of their neighbors to rejoice after he had found the one lost sheep. Likewise today the heavens are rejoicing each time one more person has come out of the wilderness.

## *In the Wilderness*

In formulating this story Jesus uses terms and ideas that are familiar to his audience: sheep and wilderness. The Hebrew word for "wilderness," *midbar,* is literally translated as a place without word or a place where there is no thing. A wilderness is a dry and barren place. The Hebrew title for the Book of Numbers is *bamidbar* meaning "in the wilderness." This book recounts the journey of the Israelites in the wilderness. Though the daily lives of our ancestors may have been dry and barren as a result of slavery, they physically went into wilderness places in order to find spiritual home. The wilderness often offers an opportunity for an encounter with God. From Abraham to Sojourner Truth, people have encountered God in the wilderness. The slaves deliberately went into the wilderness, the swamps, and the woods, away from the institutional church that dehumanized them to create an "invisible church" in the hush arbor to find acceptance and grace in God's community.

> **"When dark come, de men folks wud hang up a wash pot, bottom up'ards, in de little brush chu'ch house us hed, so's it'd catch de noise an' de oberseer wudn' hear us singin' an' shoutin.'"**
> **(Clara Young, ex-slave)**

In singing "Come Out de Wilderness" they spoke to the liberation of their souls, asking, "How did it feel when you came out of the wilderness of sin and darkness and into the light of salvation and the love of God?" Here though they were physically enslaved, their hearts, minds and spirits could be free through the love of Christ. In this they could rejoice even though their lives in chattel slavery were grim and uninspired. Their lives in Christ offered peace and joy and the promise of liberation if not on this side of glory, then perhaps on the other. They, too, like those lost sheep in Luke 15 might one day be found and brought home.

The wilderness is an alien concept for most city dwellers. Nevertheless, while they live in urban and rural areas across America and enjoy every kind of modern convenience, many people still live in a wilderness of sorts. Physically, wilderness is deserted and desolate places, deep dark woods, or lonely, cold spaces uninhabited by human beings. The wilderness conjures up images of trees and woodlands, of faraway and forgotten places. Even so, many people today are living, working, playing, sleeping, eating, hanging out, and dwelling in spiritual wilderness.

Some live in the wilderness of isolation, mixed up in the crowd but feeling alone. Some live in the wilderness of disease and sickness. Despite countless medical advancements, they still battle illness and depression. Some live in the wilderness of substance abuse and addiction, doing the same thing over and over again and expecting different results, which is the definition of insanity. Some abide in the wilderness of sin, living one way by day and another by night. Some live in the wilderness of confusion, trying to follow parents, teachers, preachers, leaders and friends who teach "do as I say, not as I do." Some stay in the wilderness of heartbreak, disappointment and dismay caused by feelings of abandonment. While many have overcome and are overcoming, there is still a "mighty long way" to travel to the door of liberation that leads out of the wilderness.

## *Come Out of the Wilderness*

There is an avenue of enlightenment and a pathway of hope that leads out of the wilderness. Likewise there is a bridge to a better day that beckons us to the other side from oppression to freedom and out of the wilderness. This spiritual song implies that a person can take initiative and come out of the wilderness. Sometimes you can put your self out of your own misery and cause a shift in the winds of change in your own life. Often it is as simple as changing your mind. Sometimes it's as simple as deciding to do something about your circumstances and finding some determination in your own heart—with the help of God—to bring about a change in your life. Sometimes it's as simple as opening the door to your own liberation and coming out of the wilderness!

And, once you have come out of the wilderness, don't forget to tell somebody how good it felt when you came out. As the song says, "Tell me how did you feel when you come out de wilderness?" Give me a description of what it felt like when you finally received your sight. Tell me how it feels to bask in the bright light of your salvation. How does it feel to walk in the cool breeze of newly found freedom? What is it like to dwell in the warmth of the love of God? Tell me how does it feel? And, remember to give your testimony to somebody so they, too, can be inspired to come out of the wilderness.

God's people are still in need of coming out of the wilderness. Many are still wandering here and there, as Paul said, "tossed to and fro and blown about by every wind of doctrine" (Ephesians 4:14). God's Word is available to all. We need only read it, learn it, apply it, and then follow it. In the story Jesus relates that the shepherd left the ninety-nine sheep, and went to find the one. In John 10:11, Jesus says, "I am the good shepherd." The search of the shepherd is a personification of God's constant calling of grace on and into our lives. We can attempt to leave from the grace of God, but the grace will not leave us. In the wilderness, Jesus will lift you on his shoulders and carry you to safety.

Like the shepherd in the parable, Jesus is concerned about the whole world— sinners—those of us who cannot live up to the rules. Jesus is constantly searching for sinners—people whom others have forgotten and written off. The diligent search and the joy the shepherd has over the one lost sheep reveals Jesus' redefinition of community and who belongs. Community is not defined by one's social standing, but by the love and grace of God. Grace brings people into community, the church, the Body of Christ. Jesus' desire is for everyone to come out of the wilderness into a community that leans on his grace.

Christians should follow the example of Jesus and be good shepherds, seeking the lost, and rejoicing and welcoming sinners into the fold. Although Jesus refers to the remainder of the ninety-nine sheep as having no need of repentance because they are righteous (verse 7), the irony underlining the parable is that none are righteous.

All have sinned and fallen short of God's glory (Romans 3:23). We are all in need of God's grace. We should party when someone has encountered God in the wilderness and chosen to lean on the shoulders of Jesus Christ.

## *A Safe Harbor*

The Black Church has largely been a sustaining force in the black community from slavery to present day drawing from a rich African heritage of singing and praying their way through life's storms. Often through sheer necessity, they have taken negative circumstances and turned them into positive results. The hush arbor is such an example. Our ancestors went deep into the wilderness to seek the spirit of God, gain their salvation, and revive their souls. The hush arbor is where many in the slave community accepted Jesus Christ. Surrounded by a community of love and acceptance, individuals could come to Christ and feel safe from the ravages of life. This phenomenon is at the heart of their survival and has yielded a kind of spiritual genius.

Resilience has been born out of that genius, cultivated by parlaying pain and suffering into hope and trust in a God who would be both willing and able to bring the people out of spiritual wilderness, leaning on the Lord. In the twenty-first century people still need a place where they can lick their wounds, where somebody will look at them and smile. In a world of domestic and international terrorism, young people and old need a place that energizes them to bounce back from wilderness living into abundant living. Our churches should be like the hush arbor where people can come out the wilderness to a place where love and acceptance reign.

## *Food for Thought*

1. *Paying taxes is a fact of modern life. Why were tax collectors in biblical times considered sinners?*

2. *In what tangible ways can you celebrate your salvation?*

3. *How does Christian salvation facilitate freedom for the mind, body, and soul?*

4. *When Christianity was offered to those who were enslaved, many embraced it while others did not. What elements of the faith do you think appealed to new believers during slavery even though it was offered to them by their oppressors?*

# References


*Bullwhip Days, The Slaves Remember: An Oral History,* James Mellon, editor (Weidenfeld & Nicolson, 1988)

*"somebody's CALLING my name" black sacred music and SOCIAL CHANGE,* by Wyatt Tee Walker (Judson Press, 1979)

*The Chronological History of the Negro in America*, by Bergman and Bergman, (Mentor Books, 1969)

*Unchained Memories: Readings From the Slave Narratives,* based on the HBO documentary (Bullfinch Press, 2002)


Consubstantiation body + blood are along side of the elements

Transubstantiation – once elements are consecrated the bread becomes body and wine becomes blood –

we would become canaballis[m]

doctrine – of church is different –

between d

1054 eastern orthodox said Jesus was not son of God –

Dogma – what we practice

beliefs + practices are what cause difference in denominations –